Alfred's
INSTRUMENTAL
CD+ INSIDE
PLAY-ALONG

Easy Top of the Charts Playlist
INSTRUMENTAL SOLOS

Arranged by Bill Galliford and Ethan Neuburg

Recordings produced by Dan Warner, Doug Emery and Lee Levin

D0809107

Contents

© 2017 Alfred Music
All Rights Reserved. Printed in USA.

ISBN-10: 1-4706-3853-3
ISBN-13: 978-1-4706-3853-5

Alfred

Alfred Cares. Contents printed on environmentally responsible paper.

7 YEARS

Words and Music by
LUKAS FORCHHAMMER, MORTEN RISTORP,
STEFAN FORREST, DAVID LABREL,
MORTEN PILEGAARD and CHRISTOPHER BROWN

7 Years - 2 - 1

Track 4: Demo
Track 5: Play-Along
mp3

CAKE BY THE OCEAN

Words and Music by
JUSTIN TRANTER, ROBIN FREDRIKSSON,
MATTIAS LARSSON and JOE JONAS

Driving dance beat (♩ = 120) 5 *Verse:*

Cake by the Ocean - 2 - 2

Track 6: Demo
Track 7: Play-Along

HEATHENS

Words and Music by
TYLER JOSEPH

7

JUST LIKE FIRE

Track 8: Demo
Track 9: Play-Along

Words and Music by
OSCAR HOLTER, MAX MARTIN,
SHELLBACK and ALECIA MOORE

Moderate rock (♩ = 82)

RIDE

Track 10: Demo
Track 11: Play-Along

Words and Music by
TYLER JOSEPH

Bright reggae (♩ = 152)

RISE

Words and Music by
KATY PERRY, MAX MARTIN,
ALI PAYAMI and SAVAN KOTECHA

Track 12: Demo
Track 13: Play-Along

Moderately (♩ = 100)

SETTING THE WORLD ON FIRE

Track 14: Demo
Track 15: Play-Along

Words and Music by
MATT JENKINS, JOSH OSBORNE
and ROSS COPPERMAN

Moderately (♩ = 94)

Track 16: Demo
Track 17: Play-Along

ONE CALL AWAY

Words and Music by
MATTHEW PRIME, JUSTIN FRANKS,
CHARLIE PUTH, BREYAN ISAAC,
MAUREEN MCDONALD and SHY CARTER

One Call Away - 2 - 1

Track 18: Demo
Track 19: Play-Along

THY WILL

Words and Music by
HILLARY SCOTT, EMILY WEISBAND
and BERNIE HERMS

Thy Will - 2 - 1

Track 20: Demo
Track 21: Play-Along

WE DON'T TALK ANYMORE

Words and Music by
CHARLIE PUTH, SELENA GOMEZ
and JACOB KASHIR

We Don't Talk Anymore - 2 - 1

YOU'LL BE BACK

(from the Broadway musical *Hamilton*)

Words and Music by
LIN-MANUEL MIRANDA

You'll Be Back - 2 - 1

STARVING (UNTIL I TASTED YOU)

Words and Music by
ANASTASIA WHITEACRE, ROBERT McCURDY,
CHRISTOPHER PETROSINO and MICHAEL TREWARTHA